Investing for Teenagers

By A Teenager

Investing for Teenagers

By A Teenager

Evan Apte
Aidin Apte

Book design by: Carolyn Vaughan (carolyn.j.vaughan@gmail.com)

Table of Contents

Chapter 1

Who Am I and What do I Know?

Hello to my GenZ friends! I am Evan, a junior at John Burroughs School in St. Louis. I have always been passionate about business. When I was younger, I woke up one day and thought that I had found my calling in life: to own a professional sports team. Why a sports team? Because, at its core, it has so many elements of a complex business operation, as well as the front office excitement that sports provide to the masses. Having played soccer and practiced Judo for most of my formative years, it likely left an indelible imprint on my psyche, fueling this interest.

Sports have been so integral to my life that I cannot imagine myself without them. They teach discipline, how to work with teams, interpersonal relationships, and how to compete within an organization and thrive in adverse environments.

When I mentioned my career goal to my parents, they were supportive, but jokingly suggested that I was born in the wrong family when it comes to such an endeavor. I started researching what they meant and quickly realized the required capital for purchasing a sports team, and I laughed too after seeing the ludicrous prices! My interest in business continues, and it has expanded into many areas: sports business, manufacturing, international operations, and investment banking. I realize that there is a whole world out there under the business rubric. I also realized that I knew so little about this world and that actually excited me, because it ignited my passion to pursue a career in business.

In the short term, I want to:

> pursue an undergraduate degree in business, where I will learn what the terms finance, economics, accounting, and health care management mean beyond the textbook definitions.

I come from a family of immigrants, both of whom worked incredibly hard to pursue careers in healthcare. They always talked about the rigorous training they underwent to build their careers, but as someone interested in the financial workings of the free markets, I have always felt something was missing. I had to learn about our country's economic systems on my own: the nation's unique laissez-faire economics, championed by figures such as Adam Smith and Milton Friedman. Growing up, these figures were my heroes, inspiring me to put my dream of owning a sports team as a major childhood inspiration, but the more I learned, the quicker it became just that: a childhood fantasy.

My parents' journey made me realize that you must put in effort to attain your goals. In sports, we always hear coaches say, 'no pain, no gain', or 'success is 99% perspiration and 1% inspiration', or 'it is a zero-sum game' and I think I have grasped these concepts. Pursuing your career dreams requires perseverance. After all, I was always a Ronaldo fan as a child because I was inspired by his workrate despite being so much older than many of his peers.

The journey is long, and you have to be willing to put in the time. My parents tell me that I may discover my true passion through my formal education and life experiences. I am doing this through diverse internships and opportunities that expose me to various aspects of business. I also watch and read articles that help me understand both academic and real-world business concepts better.

So why a book about investing for teenagers? First, because I am a teenager and most my age tend to only listen to influences their age. Second, understanding money and how to manage it is perhaps the most important concept one should understand. I also hear my parents often say that they were so focused on studying medicine and dentistry that they knew nothing about money or the business of medicine and that they wish they knew then what they know now to help set up their futures.

The fundamental factor is timing: a chance conversation I had with my parents about the 'rule of 72' when I received a cash gift from my grandparents on my birthday. Of course, as you may expect, I immediately wanted to spend it on whatever fashionable thing I had seen on Instagram. As most teenagers do, I wanted to choose the path of temporary pleasure over long-term gratification. This is where, as much as parents hate screentime, I was glad that I had TikTok and Instagram because either as a whim or out of curiosity, or whatever the reason, I looked up this unfamiliar 'rule of 72' and something just clicked (more on that later). I was hooked! I wanted to know everything I could about investing, even though I had no money to invest and did not know what that meant. The concepts of delayed gratification that parents talk about were so nebulous that I would relegate them to background white noise until I began to understand how these concepts within investing also apply to other aspects of life, delaying instant rewards for future success, the discipline to stay the course, building the resilience to weather adverse market conditions, and above all ignoring the cacophony of experts that peddle investing advice every day on social media and mainstream media outlets.

My goal with this book is to share the little that I have learned with my fellow teens and hope that it may help someone with their life journey. I fully understand that I have had a privileged and sheltered life so far, and do not claim to understand the struggles that children who live in adverse socioeconomic or geopolitical environments face, but I do believe that I have an appreciation for life challenges that others face, and I am aware of how this book may not apply to everyone. Having said that, an understanding of how achieving financial freedom, not wealth, offers you the independence to pursue your life dreams is important for everyone. I don't know where life will take me, but I am excited about the journey, and I feel that just understanding how to invest and how money grows has made me a more confident person and reinforced my passion for the world's markets.

I do not claim to know everything, but I am taking this opportunity to share something that I knew nothing about, but have learned over the past couple of years. If this book serves as a launching pad for another teen or sparks an interest in a niche area of finance or investing, this book will have achieved its desired goal. I hope you enjoy this journey through my growth as an investor. I was also fortunate that I was able to work on this book with my older brother Aidin, it was truly a bonding experience.

Chapter 2

The Rule of 72

Huh? What the heck? That was my first thought when I heard my parents ask me if I knew what the rule of 72 meant. Was it the average temperature in the fall or some new diet that they had heard about or an exercise regimen? Well, I found out that it was none of the above.

No one knows the actual origin of the term, but according to Wikipedia, my source for important information (haha!), the term is attributed to Luca Pacioli (1147-1517), an Italian mathematician and collaborator of the famous painter and Renaissance genius Leonardo da Vinci. Pacioli referred to the term in his mathematics book, *Summa de arithmetica*, to describe the concept of the doubling of an investment. Although he refers to it, he does not derive the rule, suggesting that the rule of 72 predates him.

So, how does it work, and why was I fascinated by it? Let's take the example of my $100 birthday gift. If I purchased a video game subscription or went to the amusement park for the day … instant gratification and fun, poof! The $100 is well spent but gone!

How about if I invested the money in something (more on stocks, bonds, and other investments later) that earned an average interest rate of 8% per year? The rule of 72 allows me to calculate not just how much time it will take to double my money on average, but also how much I will have in a certain period of time. For simplicity, we won't take into consideration taxes and fees for now.

So here is the rule in its simplest form. You take the number 72 and divide it by the interest, and it gives you the number of years that it will take for your money to double. There are other rules, such as the rule of 70 for calculating your money's buying power i.e. the effect of

inflation and the rule of 69, which is more accurate for continuous compounding, and even more fancy formulas for periodic compounding, but that is too much information for me and too much information gives me a headache.

So,

Doubling time = 72 / interest rate

In this thought exercise, the doubling time for my $100 would be:

72 / 8 = 9 years

Taking this further, Evan will have:

$100 at age 16
$200 at age 25
$400 at age 34
$800 at age 43
$1600 at age 52
$3200 at age 61
$6400 at age 70

Oh no .. 70! That is VERY OLD, but when I did these numbers on my calculator, I could not believe what happens to a $100 bill as it simply grows through the power of compounding with time.

That made me watch a few more TikTok videos before I realized that I need to understand the concepts of investing better so that I can get a sense of what my parents were talking about.

Thus began my investing journey. I don't know a lot, but I have learned about a few things that apply to me as a teenager, and so I thought that I could put pen to paper and share my thoughts.

———∽∽∽———

Chapter 3

Establishing the Framework (Ground Rules)

What will this book discuss? And what will it not cover?

As you can imagine, I am just a high schooler (and my brother a college freshman) and don't claim to know anything about investing, and this book is certainly not meant to provide any investment advice. However, this book serves to highlight my personal experience and what I have learned over the last couple of years. I hope that it serves as a catalyst for others to dig deeper and find a path that works for them through other readings and conversations.

In this book, I hope to outline in broad terms the types of investments, such as stocks, bonds, cash or speculative; the investment strategies, such as active or passive; the importance of understanding diversification, and the impact of the long time horizon that teenagers have on their strategy. Given my limited knowledge, I will not discuss individual plans or microstrategies and a majority of the content will focus on the concepts that I have come to understand and a buy-and-hold approach that I think is appropriate for everyone but especially for teenagers who have a very long investing time horizon.

By the end of this book, I hope to leave with you what is some useful information about investing for education, saving for retirement, varieties of accounts that minors have access to, and investing in, taxable accounts outside of retirement, even though most teenagers do not have the income stream to support some of these avenues.

The overarching purpose of this book is the hope that this will spur an interest in some teenagers to learn more from their parents and the large body of information available through social media and books on the topic. Once again, I am not qualified to talk about finance at a professional level and this book is not meant to give financial advice, but rather to try and stimulate a community of motivated teenagers who will understand the importance of paying attention to their finances earlier in life, especially given our national debt and resource challenges that are going to burden our generation as we enter adulthood. I will also only focus on investment vehicles and avenues that are most pertinent to teenagers.

An important point to note: teenagers are minors, and as such we have limited rights or ability to make our own decisions. So, as we read more about investing and managing money, we have to remember that our decision-making is dependent on our parents helping us set up many of these accounts and supporting us in our efforts to become more responsible. We should also never forget that the source of our capital to invest will often come from them too! So, if you need another excuse to be respectful and nice to your parents, which you should be anyway, use this as a really good reason!

Chapter 4

Investing in Yourself

Warren Buffett, aka the Oracle of Omaha, is one of the greatest investors of all time. He is often asked for the best advice that he can give young people, and he always says the same thing ... invest in yourself, it is the best investment you will ever make. The best investment we can make as teenagers is in our education. Although the cost of higher education, including undergraduate and graduate degrees have increased astronomically, most studies that follow lifetime earnings potential, demonstrate that college graduates and those with graduate degrees have not just a higher earning potential in their first job, but that their lifetime earning potential is significantly higher than those without a college degree. Not surprisingly, this generally applies to every level of education.

Those with college degrees earn more than those with an associate degree, and both those groups earn on average more than a high school graduate. As you can imagine, those at the bottom of the rung are those without a high school diploma. This does not mean that those who want to pursue trade schools and not higher education should not do so, but it is important in general to understand the financial implications of a lack of education.

My parents and grandparents have always highlighted to me the importance of education. They always stressed that the purpose of an education was to understand the world and its historical context better, and to become a better person who will contribute to society, whether as a doctor, teacher, public servant, or firefighter. Education opens your eyes and your mind and gives you a perspective that you would otherwise lack. Even though I am a junior in high school, I am so grateful to my teachers for the opportunities that they have provided me.

The reality remains that, given the national trends over the past several decades, it is unlikely that the cost of education will decrease in the foreseeable future. In recent years, several universities have offered need blind admissions and support for students who come from limited financial backgrounds, and there are federal, state and private programs such as loans and Pell grants that students with additional financial needs may utilize. Having said this, it is critically important to financially prepare for higher education.

So, before we spend time on the types of investments and various available strategies, let's spend some time discussing how and why to invest for education. Once again, this is something your parents may already be doing. Still, it is important to remember that it is much better to save and invest for education in a tax-advantaged account than in a taxable account.

Why is that? When your parents receive their paycheck, it is taxed by their employer based on their tax rates. As such, if they are saving for your education, the accounts that they may be using, whether they are brokerage accounts (more on this later) or savings accounts (like a bank or credit union), are taxable accounts and the money is considered 'post-tax money'. This is great but for the reasons highlighted below, from a tax and growth standpoint, it is not an ideal strategy.

In 1996, the U.S. Congress created 'qualified tuition programs' under section 529 of the Internal Revenue Code. These are called 529 College Savings Programs. Any adult can start a 529 account for college education and designate a beneficiary of the savings. The beneficiary can be another family member.

You get the idea! So what's the difference? Money saved in a 529 account is tax-advantaged in that it can grow tax-free and can be withdrawn for college or graduate school tuition, and legitimate educational expenses in other non-traditional educational programs without any additional taxes. A free lunch? Yes, but remember the word 'legitimate.' In addition, if you are the beneficiary and did not use all the money, the beneficiary can be changed by the account holder, in this case, your parent.

Many states will also provide your parent a deduction or credit on their state income taxes for contributions to a 529 account (subject to certain limits and restrictions). The 529 funds can be used for college and graduate school tuition, qualified expenses such as computers, registered apprenticeships, and most recently for private K-12 tuition, textbooks, tutoring, standardized fees and certain other qualified expenses. In 2026, the limit on K-12 expenses is $20,000.

So here's the deal; this is truly the best investment you can make in your future, but given that you are likely not making enough money, this is really the best investment your parents or grandparents can make in you. And guess what? As I mentioned above, if you don't end up using your 529 funds because you got a full-ride scholarship, or you didn't end up going to college, the beneficiary can be changed, and there will be no penalties or loss of capital.

There is a lot of information available on 529 plans depending on the state that you live in. They vary in investment choices and expenses, as well as the tax credits available, so if you are convinced, you can check out most state websites for additional information. For example, the program in my state is called Missouri's 529 Education Plan (MOST). For those who live in tax-free states such as Texas or Florida, the 529 plan is still the best thing for education, you just don't get any state tax credits, but that's fair because — guess what? You don't pay any state taxes. Some states only give tax credits for their own 529 plan, so depending on where you are, it is important to decide which is the best plan for your family. Most plans also offer a wide variety of investment choices, and the discussion in subsequent chapters regarding types of investment applies to 529 accounts too.

One disclaimer: there are other education accounts, such as Coverdell Education Savings Accounts (ESA) that are different from 529 accounts. These include contribution limitations based on income, contributions have to be placed into the account before the beneficiary turns 18, and withdrawals have to occur before the beneficiary turns 30. An advantage is that ESA's do not have withdrawal limitations for qualified expenses. Based on my reading, 529 plans are broader in scope and flexibility, but there is a lot of material available and free online for those who wish to explore these programs further. The new Trump accounts may offer additional savings options that families should explore as they are somewhat different in scope.

Chapter 5

Investing under the
influence of — Taxes

This chapter may not be the most important for a teenager with pocket money to invest, but I think understanding the where, when, and how to invest your money, and how taxes can influence these decisions, is important at every point of your life and at every income level. As Benjamin Franklin said, " In this world, nothing can be said to be certain, except death and taxes". The term " A penny saved is a penny earned" is also attributed to him.

Here are some basic ways that adults invest their money and although I may miss some categories, this covers what is important to us, teenagers.

Tax-Advantaged Accounts

1. Individual: Brokerage accounts set up by an individual for retirement savings into a vehicle such as an individual retirement account (IRA)

2. Employer-sponsored: 401K plans to save for retirement; they can come in many flavors such as 457b, 457 and 403b for non-profits and others.

3. For small business and self-employed

a. Simplified Employee Pension (SEP) IRA
b. SIMPLE (Savings Incentive Match Plan
for Employees) IRA

4. Healthcare

a. Retirement Medical Savings Accounts
b. Health Savings Accounts

Taxable Accounts

1. Savings and Checking Accounts
2. Brokerage Accounts outside of Retirement Accounts

I am biased about how teenagers should invest: they should be putting their limited income into retirement accounts, as their investment time horizon is decades, and they can thus benefit from the tax-free gains in certain types of accounts. If you are a teenager who has hit it big in AI or some other business venture, this book is clearly not for you. You certainly do not need any advice from a teenager like me who is speaking to peers who earn a little money at home or through summer jobs and internships.

So, if you think that this book is too simple, you are correct! It does not apply to adults with jobs or teenagers with substantial income.

Chapter 6

Where do we Start?

Most teenagers do not have full-time jobs as we are hopefully in school. However, many of us have jobs that generate revenue; whether it is for doing chores at home (dog walking, yardwork, and cleaning are examples) or helping in the family business part-time or in summer jobs at the library, as a lifeguard or working in local businesses. Some have full-time jobs that they maintain after school and on weekends because their families need the financial help.

What teenagers should and can do with the money they earn depends on their financial needs, but the lessons about savings and investing are universal, even if the percentage of the income that they save may differ. There are several assumptions I am going to make: a) the typical teenager stays in the parents' household, b) is a dependent on the parents' taxes and c) is on the parents' health insurance plan.

Given the super long investment horizon for teenagers of potentially over 50 years, it makes even more sense to invest as much as possible because of the lessons of the rule of 72. Now that you have decided that saving is the best option. What type of investment strategy do you use? It does not make sense to use a checking or savings account except to keep money that you may need for short term expenses, as interest rates in those accounts are fairly low historically. Individual brokerage accounts that allow one access to a broad range of investment options makes the most sense, and multiple firms offer such accounts and have a great selection of low-fee investment options (more to follow on fees). If such brokerage accounts are opened with after-tax earnings, the investments will be in non-retirement brokerage accounts. As such, any growth in the original investment and dividends generated from the investment will be taxed at capital gains tax rates and don't benefit from the tax advantages in a retirement account.

Taxes ... again? Yes! There are different types of taxes.

Income that you earn, depending on how much money you make, is subject to federal (10-37 percent), state, and local taxes. Investment income is subject to capital gains taxes (0-37 percent) that also depends on the individual's earnings and the time duration of the investment.

For teenagers, the tax rate is likely to be their parents' tax rate. How do you escape this tax trap so that if you invest your money, you get the most out of it decades later? The best way to shelter your money from taxes is to invest in a retirement account. For most teenagers, the IRA mentioned earlier is the best vehicle. In 2025, the contribution limit for a given tax year is $7000, which usually far exceeds the income most teenagers earn each year. If you are one of those teenagers who exceeds this limit, you are already doing something right, and you will have access to other retirement vehicles or taxable accounts, and we won't really discuss those other options here.

Once you make the decision to invest in an IRA, the next important decision is to consider whether to invest in a traditional IRA or a Roth IRA. They are both tax-advantaged accounts, but there is a major difference; while traditional IRAs offer an upfront or immediate tax deduction for that income year; withdrawals are taxed in retirement. What this means is that if you invest 100% of your $5000 income in a traditional IRA, you will be able to deduct your entire income for the year 2025 (depending on the complexity of your parents tax situation). But, if you withdraw the money at age 65 or after for retirement purposes, and the money has grown to $50,000 or $500,000, the entire amount is subject to applicable taxes at withdrawal. On the other hand, Roth IRA contributions are made with after-tax dollars, and one does not get an upfront tax deduction. What Roth IRAs offer is tax-free growth and tax-free withdrawals, which is amazing. In the same scenario as above, you would pay taxes on the initial $5000, but the $50,000 or $500,000 that this grows to by the time of retirement is not subject to additional taxes.

In general, for teenagers who have such a long time horizon to grow their money, in my opinion, it makes most sense to invest in a Roth IRA. Another advantage of investing in a retirement account is that you are not tempted to withdraw money, as there are penalties associated with early withdrawal before you reach the age 59 1/2 . These are general rules, and there are exceptions for early withdrawal. Still, in general, if you withdraw early, there is a 10% penalty in addition to ordinary income taxes on the IRA savings. This deterrent will keep you honest and focused on the long term.

Chapter 7

Is It Easy?

In my opinion, once you decide that investing is for you and that investing in a retirement account makes a lot of sense, then yes, the rest is somewhat easy.

First, you need to make a written plan and commit to what you are going to do, and sign it so that anytime you have doubts about your plan, you can look at your written commitment and why you are doing it to keep you on track. Then, you focus on the nuts and bolts of establishing an account and deciding on an investment strategy. To make it simple, and based on the rationale I discussed earlier, you are saving for the long term.

You have a long runway with multiple possible doublings of your money, so you should make all your investments in a retirement account. If your teenage income exceeds the limits of what you can invest in a retirement account, then you are truly an anomaly, and can talk to your parents or a trustworthy financial advisor, or both.

Why a retirement account? Simply because your invested money will grow in a tax-deferred manner. In addition, you should invest in a Roth IRA account. Why? Once again, even if the money you invest is after-tax i.e. it is taxed as ordinary income prior to investing, the money grows tax-free as opposed to tax-deferred. In a tax-deferred retirement account such as a traditional IRA, although the money grows tax-deferred, it is taxed upon withdrawal in retirement, while the Roth savings is not taxed. That's literally as close as you can get to being given free money. Of course, you cannot withdraw from these accounts willy-nilly as you will have to pay penalties and taxes, but that is the whole point! You do not want to withdraw; you want to use your youth to let this money grow.

So now that you have decided to invest in your future with the small but valuable capital that you have, in the next chapter, let's discuss where you can deploy it.

Chapter 8

Choices, Choices, More Choices

To invest your money, you need to open an investment account. There are several low-cost brokerage firms that you can use, such as Vanguard, Schwab, or Fidelity. I personally use Vanguard, but you can research what makes sense for you.

Typically, you open a money market account here, which serves as a checking account to hold your money, and depending on the account type, you can also earn some interest on that money. This is not your primary investment vehicle, but the place from which you can deploy the funds into other accounts. Basically, a piggy bank.

Let's talk a little bit about the types of investments. There are a dizzying number of choices, and so it is essential to establish the ground rules ... or at least the ground rules that I have established for myself.

Passive versus active investing strategies: The first decision to make is whether you want to invest in individual stocks, actively managed funds or passively managed index funds.

These decisions are personal, and I will just tell you what I do and have learned, once again, from smart people such as Warren Buffett. When he was asked what you would recommend to a regular person who is investing for themselves and for their retirement, he said that he would recommend that they invest in a low-cost, passively managed index fund.

Let's explore this further. Why not invest in individual stocks? Stock markets in the developed world are considered relatively efficient. Therefore, the wisdom of millions of investors and analysts usually determines the stock price, and the variables are mostly accounted for. The ability of an individual investor, especially a novice teenager, to consistently beat the market by thinking that they are more innovative than the big firms that spend millions on analyzing companies is essentially zero.

So picking individual stocks is a loser's game. How about choosing a financial advisor to do this for you, or choosing a stock mutual fund (which is like a basket of stocks) actively managed by someone?

It has been shown repeatedly by brilliant people like Larry Swedroe that after accounting for fees and evaluating performance over the long term, actively managed funds and advisors who charge exorbitant fees underperform passively managed, low cost index funds.

Let's cut to the chase and then dig deeper: I believe that the best choice for a teenager investing for the long term is to invest in a low-cost stock index fund or a life cycle fund. To understand what this means, we will have to discuss some types of investments that are available, and why this strategy is not the only strategy, but it is the most logical.

Chapter 9

Off Topic

Before I dig into the various options available for investing such as stocks, bonds, commodities, other speculative investments and things I am unaware of, please let me digress in order to highlight how I concluded what teenagers should do. Again, I am not an accountant or financial advisor, but based on what I have learned, my philosophy is a good option, and it works for me.

There are a few things that may be relevant to the choices I think are right for teenagers who are not dependent on their earned income for survival or sustenance. So, if you are one of the fortunate teens who do not have to worry about spending $10 at Starbucks, hundreds of dollars for school supplies and maybe even more for school tuition, you should thank your parents immediately, and then realize that this applies to you. You can essentially make an informed decision to save your 'pocket' money towards your retirement. A bonus will be that your parents will be proud that you are demonstrating maturity and responsibility, and who knows, maybe they may match some of your efforts!

Here are a few important terms for mastering markets..

Liquidity: This is a term used to indicate money that is easily accessible, such as in your bedside drawer or your checking account. If you are a teenager who fits the description above, your need for liquidity is non-existent as your parents are your liquidity. You should be focused on investing for the long term and be prepared to take higher risks that come with market fluctuations as your time horizon is almost infinite … not really, but you get the point.

Risk: This is tied into liquidity. As your need for liquidity is minimal, your risk tolerance should be higher.

Greed: In the context of greed, the biblical book of Ecclesiastes states that it is better to sleep well than to eat well. Investing should always be done with this simple concept in mind.

Ignore the Noise: Once you get into the habit of investing, have a written plan and stick to it, the most important thing to do is ignore the noise. Whether it is another kid at school saying how much money they have made on a stock that they bought last month or the next Instagram tip that you see claiming that someone had discovered the formula to quadruple your investment overnight, just remind yourself of your signed commitment to yourself and realize that none of this applies to you. If someone had truly discovered the magic potion to quadruple their money overnight, would they tell everyone on Instagram?

Chapter 10

Types of Investments:
Good and Bad Choices

There are many types of investments that you can make with your savings. Some are traditional and time-tested, others not so much, and those are called speculative or alternative investments. The options are myriad, some very complex, and beyond my pay grade, so I will stick to the ones I know and the ones I think most people hear about. As the saying goes, simplicity is the essence of beauty.

Traditional
1. Stocks
2. Bonds
3. Mutual funds
4. Exchange Traded Funds
5. Real Estate
6. Cash

Speculative
1. Cryptocurrencies
2. Junk bonds
3. Commodities
4. Venture capital
5. Private equity

For the purposes of this book, we will ignore speculative or alternative investments because teenagers should definitely not be in that part of the world, as it is definitely not their sandbox.

Let's discuss the traditional investments a little more.

What is a stock? It represents fractional ownership of a company, also called equity, the value of which fluctuates with the market value of a company. As such, you participate in the losses and the gains of the company (capital gains) and are also eligible to profit-sharing, as companies often distribute profits as dividends. Stocks are traded on public exchanges such as the New York Stock Exchange or NASDAQ. You can buy individual stocks through a brokerage account that you open, and deposit funds to trade, or a basket of stocks in a mutual fund, also offered through brokerage accounts. The value of a stock can fluctuate depending on the market valuation of the company.

What is a bond? It is essentially a fixed investment in the form of a loan (principal) from the investor to a company or a government, for a fixed period of time. In exchange for the loan, the borrower promises to pay a fixed rate of interest to the investor and return the principal after the time period has expired. Although less risky in terms of capital loss than stocks, bonds are subject to interest rate and default risk, nonetheless bonds are generally considered safer investments than stocks, but offer lower long-term returns. Bonds can be purchased from the government, corporations, municipalities, and other borrowers directly or through brokerage accounts.

Mutual funds are investment entities that pool investor money to buy multiple stocks, bonds, and other assets to allow diversification so that you can own proportional shares of the fund, which represents proportional ownership of all holdings in the fund. These funds can be very broadly diversified, such as owning holdings throughout the world or certain parts of the world, such as the US, Europe, or emerging markets and other focused regions or sectors, such as real estate, technology, and others. The funds can also be targeted to the size of the companies in the case of stock funds or the types of borrowers, such as governments, private companies, high-risk corporate borrowers, and others.

Exchange-traded funds are similar to passively invested mutual funds, but they may have some tax advantages and differences in how they are traded.

Investments in real estate can be done through individual investments that teenagers with little money will likely not have access to or through mutual funds that they can access.

It is critical to talk about **cash investments**, as this can be in the form of keeping your money in a drawer by your bedside or in checking or savings accounts in a bank, where your money makes very little interest, and the possibility of capital growth over decades is minimal. This is where the concept of inflation is important. Think of keeping cash investments as having paper money stored in a drawer with termites. Every day, a little bit of the paper will be chewed up by termites, and over time, the $100 bill will physically disappear. This is what happens to money every day.

The value of a fixed dollar amount decreases every day because of inflation, as the cost of goods and services increases over time. This is why it is so important to invest our savings in ways that multiply over the years to counteract the effects of inflation. All teenagers know how much more a McDonald's burger is now versus five years ago … that's inflation for you!

All I will say about speculative investments is that these are for gamblers or for sophisticated traders, and we should stay away from these and focus on traditional investments.

Chapter 11

A Simple Plan

P lans are never simple. And like everything else, they are hard to follow for an extended period of time. The same goes for investment plans. So here are a few simple rules to follow:

- Have a written document that you sign and date to remind yourself of your commitment.

- Try to automate your investments if possible, so that you don't forget to stick with your plan.

- Simplify your plan with a focus on investing for retirement.

Here is a strategy that can work very well for most teenagers until they get to an age where they have real jobs and would need to modify their plan.

1. The investment strategy discussed in this book is a long-term investment strategy. Teenagers have decades to allow their invested money to multiply. Stocks over this long a period of time have typically overperformed bonds, as one takes higher risks in investing in stocks versus bonds. It makes sense for a teenager's retirement investment account to have 100% stocks but a small allocation to bonds would also be reasonable.

2. Decades of research have shown that buying individual stocks is not a winning strategy, but purchasing a basket of

stocks as in mutual funds, is a better approach. An individual who buys individual stocks is unlikely to be able to consistently beat millions of investors.

3. In addition, passively managed mutual funds are low cost, containing various baskets of stocks based on the indices they replicate, and consistently outperform actively managed funds, which also have higher costs (fees). Investing money in a passively managed, low-cost index fund is thus a winning strategy.

4. There are many stock index funds; some focus on sectors such as biotechnology or health, others focus on regions such as the U.S. or emerging markets, and still others based on the size of the companies included in the index.

A smart strategy may be to invest in one or two very broad stock index funds such as a total stock index fund that seeks to mirror the entire U.S. stock market or a total international stock index fund that does the same with ex-U.S. stocks. As discussed before, you can invest in an ETF or the index fund. Should you want to have some bonds in your investment, you can allocate a small portion to a U.S. or international bond index fund.

5. You try to invest periodically at defined intervals such as monthly in a manner called dollar cost averaging (DCA). This means that you are investing a set amount of money every week or month, and are averaging out the cost of buying into your investments without risking buying only at times when the market is high. The way to do it is by establishing a money market or checking/cash account where you deposit your money and then using it to invest in your chosen retirement funds with a DCA approach. The DCA approach is akin to studying for school every day and not just cramming right before a test.

6. Parents as partners — don't forget that we are minors and need our parents to establish investment accounts for us. Our incomes as teenagers are so limited that we are likely to fall below the limits for annual Roth IRA accounts, allowing us to invest in these tax-advantaged accounts. These accounts are for investing money that we have received as income (work), allowing us to multiply money where the gains will be tax-free as long as we realize that this investment is for retirement.

Your parents can also help you create an account with the same brokerage firm, where you can invest money that is not income but cash received as birthday gifts and other gifts from family members. Investments can be made in similar types of funds, but these are taxable accounts. These accounts have names such as a Uniform Gifts to Minor Account (UGMA).

7. Show commitment to your plan and make your parents a part of that journey. You will find that they will support you not just morally, but if they see your desire to secure your future through a well-thought-out investment strategy, you may find that they come up with matching plans where they reward your efforts.

8. Don't fall for trends that you hear online or from peers. There will be many peers who talk about how much money they have made on Bitcoin or on some stock that they heard about. Stay the course; invest in low-cost, index funds or ETFs that are broadly diversified and managed passively. Just like most fashions come and go, trends in investing also come and go, and you have to remind yourself of your plan.

You got this!

Evan Apte is a Junior at John Burroughs School in St. Louis. During high school, Evan became interested in the inner workings of business, joining clubs such as Young Entrepreneurs and founding his own Sports Business club with a friend. A soccer enthusiast, Evan was also intrigued by the financial enterprises behind sports at a young age, particularly player contracts, team management, and sports agencies. He hopes to learn more about international affairs and its interconnectedness to business in his undergraduate studies.

Aidin Apte is a freshman at Washington University in St. Louis, currently studying biology and anthropology. During his time at WashU, Aidin became deeply interested in the intersection of healthcare and socioeconomics, which fueled his passion for researching how young teens can navigate financial stability as they enter adulthood.